This book was edited and published
by Lewis W. Gillenson
Designed by: Martin Rosenzweig
Associate Editor: Philip Doyle

The Boots Adams Story

by
Norman M. Lobsenz

**Phillips Petroleum Company
Bartlesville, Okla.**

CONTENTS

Warm Words From An Old Friend

I am delighted to know that the story of the life and accomplishments of my friend, Boots Adams, is to be told in a biography written as a tribute to him. Such a volume will be treasured by his contemporaries, while the story of his achievements cannot fail to be an inspiration to those who, in future years, may have an opportunity to read it.

It is most fitting that this special celebration should mark the 66th anniversary of the birth of K. S. Adams. For many years he has guided the destinies of Phillips Petroleum Company, whose "66" symbol, largely through his efforts, is now known nationwide and is becoming the mark of a worldwide company. The growth of Phillips from a small concern to one that has developed into a benefactor in many areas of human life is inseparably entwined with the dynamic career of Boots Adams. It is a notable example of foresight and hard work, bearing fruit under the free, competitive enterprise system of America.

During the years of my major postwar responsibilities, first as commander of the NATO forces and later in the White House, it was my good fortune to have Boots as a staunch friend; beyond that he was a trusted advisor whose judgment I valued highly.

A dynamic leader of industry, a willing pioneer when bold advances are the order of the day, and a devoted upholder of democracy and human betterment; these are only a few of the reasons that make a commemorative book about Boots Adams a volume to read, preserve and cherish.

With a personal salute to a man whom I deeply admire, I assure Boots of my continued affection and esteem and wish for him many more active, fruitful and happy years.

DWIGHT D. EISENHOWER
GETTYSBURG, PENNSYLVANIA 17325

The Measure of a Man

The measure of a man—the key to the mechanism that makes him tick—can often be discovered not so much in the major aspects of his life as perhaps more significantly in the small, quickly-forgotten incidents of an ordinary day. Obviously in the 66 years of Kenneth S. Adams' life, and in the 45 years during which he has served the Phillips Petroleum Company, there have been hundreds of major decisions, actions, turning points—all of which shed light on the essential character of the man. Yet one almost-forgotten and completely trivial incident seems to epitomize the essential Boots Adams.

It happened some years ago. Adams, on his way to an important business meeting, was in an automatic elevator which turned balky while he was riding to his appointment on an upper story. The car moved slowly, in fits and starts, stopping at every floor. And each time it stopped the doors would open, close half-way, open again, begin to close, bounce open—and go through this routine four or five times before they finally shut tight and the car headed upwards again.

The man who was with Adams in the elevator recalled that after two flights Adams began to get impatient; after a couple more he was kicking and shoving the car doors in an effort to get them moving; and that when there were still half a dozen floors to go, Adams suddenly flung himself out of the elevator and headed for the stairway, taking the steps two and three at a time to get where he was going.

All his life Kenneth Adams has been hurrying toward the top—finding and taking the fastest, most direct way toward a goal, whether it was a personal one or a goal for the company which has in so large a part been his life. No obstacle stands in his way for long, providing it can be overcome by hard work, the willingness to gamble, by the impetuosity to attack it head-on, by the patient accumulation of knowledge, or by the intelligence to seek alternate solutions.

The proof lies in some deceptively simple sets of facts and figures. Take a young man of 21, forced to leave college in midstream for financial reasons; he has no special training, no special skills; when he goes to work as a warehouse clerk for the Phillips Petroleum Company in the small town of Bartlesville, Oklahoma, he does not, in his own words, "know an oil well from a water well." The company itself is fairly small potatoes: a small supplier of crude oil with assets of only $3,000,000.

Yet 17 years later this same young man becomes President of the company, then one of the youngest men in the country ever to head a national corporation. Phillips, by that year of 1938, had $212,000,000 in assets, three refineries and 2,200 miles of pipelines. And today, after 27 years of guidance by Adams and his team of executive associates, the company stands eighth among America's oil corporations. It has nearly $2,000,000,000 in assets, six refineries, 8,000 miles of pipeline, and 28,000 employees; it is a producer, processor and marketer of oil and natural gas on six continents, and a leader in petrochemical production and research.

This will be the story of how Boots Adams did it.

9

They Called Him "Boots"

IN THE WHITE FRAME HOUSE at 75 South Valley Road, Kansas City, Kansas, where Kenneth Stanley Adams grew up—and where his 90-year-old mother, Mrs. Luella Stanley Adams, still lives—the staircase leading up from the front parlor starts out from a broad, two-step-high base. Not long ago Mrs. Gladys Whitehead, Kenneth Adams' older sister, was reminiscing about Boots' childhood.

"When he was a little fellow," she told me, "not even two years old, Kenneth used to climb up on those two steps over there and start talking baby talk and just go on and on. His grandmother Adams used to say, 'You know, that child is going to be a preacher or a lawyer or an important businessman when he grows up'."

In Adams' case, the child was father to the man in many ways: in energy, gregariousness, popularity, a love for and skill at sports, drive and enthusiasm, in the willingness to take risks—what his mother calls "venturesomeness"—and, of course, in the nickname which has virtually replaced his given name.

Adams was born August 31, 1899, in the small farming community of Horton, Kansas. His father, John V. Adams, was a locomotive engineer on the Rock Island railroad; his mother was the daughter of a stockman. The family moved to Kansas City when Kenneth was about a year old. When he was about three years old flood waters inundated low-lying areas of Kansas City and the Adamses gave shelter to about two dozen railroad men and their families who had been driven from their homes. Kenneth had just been given some new black leather boots with red tops, and he liked them so much he didn't want to take them off even to go to bed. The flood refugees started to call the boy "Boots," and somehow the name stuck, following him to school, to college, to Phillips—and "Boots" it still is today, whether Adams is being addressed by a friend, a business associate, or the President of the United States. "Some folks never knew his real name," says his mother. "But his Dad and I have always called him Kenneth."

Childhood was a busy and exciting time. "Something was always happening to him," his mother recalls. "He was never afraid of anything. In the summers he'd visit my brother's farm and try to ride the horses, and he used to get thrown off them regularly. He pretty nearly drowned when he was six, but he was rescued just as he was going down for the third time. Once when he was sledding, another boy ran into him

BARE FEET AT SIX *months, then,*
with sister Gladys,
high-laced shoes at two years which
preceded black boots
that gave Kenneth Adams
his nickname.
Above is Adams' childhood home
in Kansas City, Kan.

DUSTY MAIN STREET *of Everest, Kansas was site of Prescott Elementary School, which Adams attended for eight years.*

ON COLORADO VACATION, *John and Luella Adams treat four-year-old Boots and sister, Gladys to burro ride.*

AROUND THE TIME *young Adams was wearing Little Lord Fauntleroy suit, citizens of Bartlesville watched baptism from the first bridge built over the Caney River.*

and Kenneth's larynx was cracked; he couldn't talk at all for a while. Sometimes his father and I wondered if he'd live to grow up. When we got an automobile Kenneth was the first to learn to drive it. He wasn't supposed to drive while his father was away, but he did; once he broke a wheel on the auto the day his dad was coming home and, oh, my, Kenneth was a busy boy scouring around getting a new wheel to put on before his Dad got there."

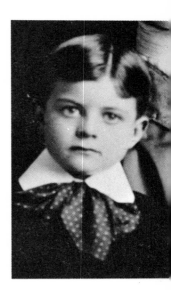

*I*t was in high school that Boots first embarked on his athletic career, starring in football, baseball and basketball. According to an old friend, Dr. John Billingsley of Kansas City, "Boots was all knees and elbows. I was a guard and he was a forward, and I was always assigned to Boots. All through the game we'd battle each other and afterwards walk off the court with our arms around each other. Boots was always highly competitive, but there wasn't anybody who didn't like him. He was a good-looking cuss, and the girls were crazy about him. And though Boots would kid his teachers the same way as he kidded everybody, he could always get away with it." Well, almost always.

In his senior year at Wyandotte High, Boots chewed up a wad of paper and flipped it at a classmate who was writing at the blackboard. As Adams tells the story, "The teacher just happened to turn the wrong way at that moment and the spitball hit him right between the eyes and knocked his glasses off. He asked who had thrown it, and I told him. 'Well,' he said, 'I'm just going to have to expel you from school.' I was sent to the principal's office and I was scared to death. But the principal was a wonderful man named William A. Bailey. He took me out of that class for a while and kept me in his office as a messenger. A few weeks later I was back in good standing again. If Bailey had allowed me to be expelled, I probably would have quit school for good."

As it was, Adams was graduated from Wyandotte High School in June, 1917, just two months after the U. S. entered World War I. Still three months shy of being old enough to enlist in the Army, Boots started the summer selling aluminum cooking utensils door-to-door to earn some of the money he would need in the Fall, when he planned to enter pre-medical school at Kansas University.

"I'll never forget the first house I approached," says Adams. "I'd picked out the biggest one in the block. It turned out the folks living there

GROWING UP. *Little boy of six matures into teenage student-athlete, is shown with parents and sisters, as Wyandotte High School basketball forward, and as member of varsity baseball team (second from right, rear row).*

YEAR OF TRANSITION *found Boots closing out high school athletic career*
as star back on football squad, then visiting his aunt and uncle in rustic area
near Bartlesville to work at a summer job.

21

PRE-ADAMS ERA *of the oil business in Oklahoma. Arrow points to first office of Phillips Petroleum in Bartlesville; checking pipe via horse-and-carriage on the Osage-Cherokee line north of Tulsa; roaring gusher on Osage oil field.*

were newlyweds, and I sold them a complete set of my stock.
My commission on that one sale alone came to $60. I guess that
was my first 'big deal'."

Later that summer Boots made what would prove to be an historic trip;
his first visit to Bartlesville, Okla., to visit his uncle and aunt, Mr. and Mrs.
George McClintock, in nearby Dewey, Okla. His primary aim was to
earn additional money. By working as a delivery man on an ice wagon
for the Crystal Ice Plant, which McClintock's brother, Harry,
owned, Adams not only got together more tuition money, but built up
his leg and stomach muscles in anticipation of going out for
freshman football and basketball.

*I*n September Adams entered Kansas U. He immediately enlisted in the
Students' Army Training Corps—the World War I equivalent of ROTC.
With his usual drive, Boots took on schoolwork and military duties,
made the basketball and football squads, and handled several part-time
jobs. He had joined Sigma Chi fraternity, and to pay for his room
and board he kept the chapter account books and stoked the furnace.
("Sixty tons of coal a month!" Boots remembers grimly.) In his "spare"
time Adams worked in the college gymnasium to earn extra cash.

In the spring of 1918 the SATC drill officer announced that there were two
openings in an Officers Training School for the Field Artillery.
Volunteering were Adams and A. D. "Dutch" Lonborg, who was a
fraternity brother and a basketball teammate. (Lonborg went on to be
head basketball coach at Northwestern University for 23 years and
recently retired after 14 years as Director of Athletics at Kansas U.)
They were sent to Camp Zachary Taylor, in Louisville, Ky., and Adams'
most vivid memory of the rail trip east is that he lost $32 of his
hard-earned money in a dice game. (An interviewer, reminding Adams of
his reputation as a winning gambler, was told—"That wasn't until
later in my life, when the stakes were higher.") One of the first things
Adams and Lonborg did at Camp Zachary Taylor was to organize
a football team.

Commissioned on October 15, 1918, for the "period of the emergency,"
Adams was honorably discharged on December 6, 1918, three weeks after
the Armistice was signed. Boots remembers feeling terribly "let down."
"I'd never been out of Kansas until the Army sent me to Kentucky,"
he says. "Now I wasn't going to see Paris after all."

WARTIME (1918) found Boots Adams
at Field Artillery Officers Training School,
Camp Zachary Taylor, Louisville, Ky.
By peacetime (1922), he was back in Bartlesville
where his sister Gladys,
(with Adams, below) came to watch
him play as star of local American
Legion Post football eleven,
(Boots is standing, top left).

Boots returned to college in the spring of 1919, this time enrolling in the School of Business since he realized he could not afford the extra years of study necessary for a medical degree. That summer and the next he went back to Bartlesville for more muscle-strengthening tours of duty on the ice wagon. Although his 12-hour-plus working days started at 4 A.M., Adams still had enough energy left in the evenings to "relax" by playing basketball in the YMCA gymnasium with a pick-up team. One of the players was a Phillips Petroleum Company employee named Bill Feist. Feist told young Adams that there were several men at Phillips who liked to play basketball. "Why don't you get a job with the company and stay in Bartlesville?" Feist suggested.

"No, thanks," Adams replied. "I'm going back to college."

But towards the end of August, when Adams was getting ready to go back to Kansas, Feist told him that there was a definite job opening at Phillips that Adams could have. It paid $125 a month.

"That's a lot of money," Adams recalls saying.

Both Boots and his parents had always dreamed of the day when he would get his college degree. But here was a chance, it seemed, to earn enough money in six months to pay for a year or more of schooling. Boots and his folks agreed that it was worthwhile trading time for money. Thus, on November 17, 1920, Boots Adams went to work for Phillips. He hasn't stopped yet.

Up
The
Ladder

ONE OF THE PAMPHLETS PUBLISHED by the American Petroleum Institute, of which Kenneth Adams is an Executive Committee member, describes for high school and college students the many career opportunities in the oil industry. This is a part of an industry-wide program to interest bright youngsters in the field and to guide them up the vocational ladder. And today, like other major oil companies, Phillips sends interviewers to college campuses to recruit outstanding prospective employees.

But when Boots Adams started his climb up the ladder, he was strictly on his own. Because he had been told that his work would be in the "warehouse," Adams reported on his first day in overalls, a blue-jean shirt and a pair of heavy workshoes. His first boss, L. E. Fitzjarrald, growled, "Where are you goin' in that get-up?"

"To work in the warehouse," Boots answered.

"Well, get your clothes changed. We don't have a warehouse like that here. We have an office."

At a huge oak desk on the fifth floor of the old First National Bank Building in Bartlesville—the three-year-old Phillips Company had two whole floors in the building then—Adams worked on material vouchers and inventory. Spurred by ambition, and realizing at the same time that he knew very little about business procedures in general or the oil business in particular, Adams became, as he puts it, "a fanatic about correspondence school courses."

Although his company working hours were from 7 A.M. until the job was done (with no pay for overtime), Boots somehow made time to master almost every business subject on which a course was available: accounting, business law, finance, business administration. The oil industry began to fascinate Adams. He wanted to learn everything about it, and so he not only studied the work of his own department, but the techniques used in all the others.

"He was an unusual fellow," remembers Fitzjarrald. "Seemed he never could learn enough. During the years he was working for me he'd never take a vacation—always said he'd rather put in the time working in some other department so he could learn how *it* operated. He liked to get out into the drilling fields, roustabouting, to see how the rigs worked. He worked as a ditch-digger, a pumper, a tool-dresser.

"One time he was out in the Burbank field on a cloudy, windy day with

EARLY DAYS ON THE JOB FOR
PHILLIPS. *Energetic young
employee Adams' tough-minded
first boss was L. E. Fitzjarrald
(above). Excitement was in the
air as oil boom filled fields
with drilling rigs.*

the rod crew. Those days, before we had rod baskets to hang them in, we
had to 'tail out' the rods—grab hold of the unscrewed rod, hook it up
and pile it outside of the derrick. Boots was tail boy on a crew this day, and
when he came back in to get a rod he happened to look up in the derrick
just when a big cloud was passing over. He thought for sure it was the rig
that was moving, instead of the cloud. 'Get out of here,' he yelled, 'this
thing's falling over!' And he took off! The boys never let Boots forget that."

In addition to learning about the company, Adams was always thinking
about ways to improve its day-to-day operations. Talk to any Phillips
employee today and it won't be long before you hear about "up-grading"—
an Adams concept which simply means getting the most and the best
out of every product and process and person. Perhaps Adams' first attempt
at up-grading occurred during that first year as a warehouse clerk.
The story is told in a letter, written some time later to Adams by his Uncle
Harry McClintock, in which the latter remembers meeting his nephew
in the Bartlesville bank:

"I had not seen you for some time past and I recall that I inquired how
everything was going with you. You replied that you liked your job. You
told me something you had been doing during your off-time hours that
interested me very much, for it indicated you were thinking not just in
terms of a 'job' but in terms of the 'company'. You stated that your
company was paying tremendous sums in premiums to insurance concerns
for carrying their risks. You mentioned that you had worked out a
plan whereby a big saving could be effected, that it was done on your own
time, and though it was not in your department of work you had handed
it to your boss to be submitted to the higher-ups for consideration. A short
time later I was talking to Mr. Phillips and I told him he had in his
employ a young fellow who was thinking in bigger terms than his job.
I told him about the risk plan you had worked out in your spare hours.
'Well,' said Mr. Phillips, surprised, 'is that where that came from?'"

*E*ven while he was working long hours, and studying in his spare
time, Boots never lost his zest for sports. For example, for several seasons
he was the star running back on the football team sponsored by the
American Legion, James H. Teel Post, in Bartlesville. In 1921 the team was
Oklahoma-Kansas champion. A yellowed newspaper clipping from that
year reports that "Boots Adams, in perfect greyhound form, gives a thrill

30

ANOTHER GUSHER! *Adams early spotted power of wasted natural gas
in gushers such as this, pioneered in harnessing natural gas as fuel.*

to the fans. His long end runs usually leave a trail of opponents spilled along the field in tribute to the fastest pair of legs on the team."

But basketball remained Boots' favorite game. For some time he had continued playing on the YMCA court with several other young Phillips employees. Then, in 1921, he got the idea of organizing them into a company team and scheduling games with other oil and supply company teams in and around Bartlesville. Rivalry ran high, and it wasn't unusual for fans in other towns to pepper the visiting Phillips players with pebbles fired by slingshots through the chicken-wire fences that bounded the playing court. The Phillips team began to take on top-rank caliber. But Frank Phillips, watching his young employees play, saw more going on, on the field, than simply a winning quintet. He noticed that in basketball as in business close teamwork and quick decisions were required. Why not, he thought, have the Phillips Company officially sponsor the team and thus keep an eye out for men of potential executive ability?

Of course the end of that story is well-known: through the years the Phillips 66ers became one of the greatest of all industrial basketball teams. Adams had to wait nearly 20 years before the 66ers won their first National Amateur Athletic Union championship in 1940—and Boots was President of the company by then. But that was to be one of the first of many national and Olympic titles for the 66ers. As a result of his long-time contribution to basketball, both as player and supporter, Adams was elected in 1958 to the Helms Athletic Foundation's Basketball Hall of Fame.

DURING HIS EARLIEST DAYS *at Phillips, Boots (shown with Dad) went into the oil fields to learn every phase of the business; how to dig pipeline ditches and to repair pipe.*

Adams' concept of a company basketball team has proved a tremendous asset in the growth of the corporation, for scores of the outstanding players who were first attracted to Phillips by the opportunity of playing on the 66ers have developed into key executives of the firm. Just as two examples, there is Paul Endacott, a former President of the company and now Vice-Chairman of the Board of Directors; he was a college basketball All-American—1923's "Player-of-the-Year"—before he joined Phillips and its team; and W. F. (Bill) Martin, several times AAU All-American with Phillips, now a Senior Vice-President recently advanced from Secretary-Treasurer.

The men who play on the team are hired not primarily for their court skills, but for their potentials as oil men. Fortunately, the same basic characteristics often underlie both talents. As Adams once said: "A man who has the alertness and the stamina to make a good basketball player also may have the qualities to make a good employee. Athletics makes for competitiveness. Our men keep at it. There's no room for deadwood on a basketball court or in a corporation. That's one of the policies that put our company where it is today."

After two years as a materials inventory record-keeper, Adams was transferred to the Production Department as Assistant to the Operations Manager. In 1926 he was moved to the Accounting Department, where he was put in charge of field payroll. Characteristically, as soon as he learned his job well enough to analyze it, he began setting up new and more efficient kinds of accounting systems. Adams continued his advanced correspondence courses in banking and business administration, and by 1927 had become assistant chief clerk in Accounting.

In six years, Boots Adams had slowly but steadily put many rungs of the ladder beneath him. Now he was about to take the first of his big steps upward.

Working With Uncle Frank

On MAY 3, 1927, O. K. WING, then Secretary and Treasurer of the company, took a sheet of blue memorandum paper from his desk drawer and wrote in blue ink the following recommendation to Frank Phillips: *"K. S. Adams has been with the company about eight years. He is now my chief assistant looking after credits, etc. He has had a fairly good education and has good potential possibilities. Has been receiving $350 per month since 1926 (Sept.) and I now recommend that his salary be increased to $400 and that he be elected to the office of Assistant Secretary and Treasurer."* Adams, of course, knew nothing of this memo. All *he* knew was that in his first personal encounter with impulsive and demanding "Uncle Frank" he had unwittingly committed a major *faux pas*. The occasion—which preceded by only two weeks the dispatch of Wing's note—had been a barbecue party given by Phillips at his Woolaroc Lodge in honor of Chief Bacon Rind, tribal head of the Osage Indians on whose land the first of the Phillips Company wells were sunk. The good-will of the Osage Indian Nation—which depended in turn on the good-will of the chief—was vital to the company. Adams had been assigned the job of checking guests arriving at the Lodge against a master invitation list.

"At one point," Adams remembers, "I was in the middle of a mass of people at the entrance, busy with a hundred details, when I noticed an elegant touring car draw up with a number of persons in it. Because there were so many cars already at the gate, this new arrival had to wait. But after a couple of minutes it maneuvered out of the line, turned and sped away. I didn't think anything of it at the time. But about an hour later Mr. Phillips came out to the gate and asked me if I'd seen anything of the guest of honor.

" 'No, I haven't, sir,' I said.

" 'Didn't you see a group of Osages in a large car?' he asked.

" 'Oh, those,' I said, with a sudden sinking feeling. 'There was a Pierce Arrow with a chauffeur and a group of Indians in it. They drove up, but they had to wait a couple of minutes because there were other cars ahead of them, so they drove away.'

"Mr. Phillips looked at me for a moment as if he was about to take my head off. Then he growled, 'Those were our guests of honor—you idiot!' "

Phillips himself drove all the way to Pawhuska to personally apologize to Chief Bacon Rind, who was sulking in his quarters and denouncing that

EARLY ERROR *at Woolaroc barbecue, when Boots inadvertently slighted Osage tribal chief, is long forgotten by the day of the golden wedding celebration of Mr. and Mrs. Frank Phillips, which was attended by offended chief's successor, Fred Lookout.*

"young upstart" who wouldn't let him in to the party. Phillips rode back to Woolaroc with the chief, there were apologies made all around, and the barbecue went on successfully. But next morning Mr. Phillips summoned Adams to his office, made him stand up during a ten-minute lecture, and ordered him to write an explanation and an apology to be transmitted to Chief Bacon Rind.

S ays Adams: "That was the first time I had ever met Frank Phillips, the first time I came to his personal attention—and I made *some* impression." Uncle Frank, who never forgot anything, was still miffed about the incident when Wing's memo reached him, and not inclined to put much credence in Adams' abilities to do anything properly. Phillips, however, was assured that Adams was the right man for the job even if he couldn't recognize a guest of honor when he saw one. Nevertheless, when the memo was returned to Wing with the scribbled notation, "O.K., Ex. Comm., F. P." there had been some changes made in it: the words "and Treasurer" had been crossed out, and the suggested new salary of $400 had been marked down to $375. Only a year later, however, Adams was also given the post of Assistant Treasurer, marking the onset of his association with the executive staff of the corporation. And a few months after that Phillips wrote a letter to Boots Adams that not only indicated all was forgiven but accurately forecast the shape of things to come. Adams, in dealing with businessmen who called on him during the day, had been, over and above his regular duties, selling them several hundred dollars' worth of "Coupon Books" good for discount purchases of gas and oil at Phillips' service stations. Most of them, of course, would remain Phillips' customers long after the coupons were used up. Frank Phillips learned of this and wrote Adams: "I am taking this opportunity to express to you my appreciation of the spirit and initiative that has led you to go beyond your regular duties to further the interests of our company. Such a spirit throughout our organization could not help but insure for us a tremendous success in any field we choose to enter." In 1932 Adams and Phillips were riding the train together back to Bartlesville from a business trip to New York. In the dining car one evening Uncle Frank casually informed Boots that at the next meeting of the Board of Directors he was going to recommend that Adams be made his "assistant."

WORKING WITH UNCLE FRANK *was a full-time job. Adams aided Frank Phillips with administrative details, joined him at Bartlesville airfield to welcome Saudi Arabian officials who came to discuss overseas oil venture.*

"For a moment," Adams told me, "I was aghast. For one thing, what I thought he meant by 'assistant' was just a glorified secretary. And I had seen some of Uncle Frank's secretaries and assistants as they passed through our company. Why, some of them had lasted as long as six months in the job before they vanished from sight. I didn't want what I thought was a promising career to end that way. So I said, 'You know, Mr. Phillips, I can't take dictation or type very well.' He looked at me over the rim of his glasses and said, 'I don't mean *secretary*, young man, I mean *assistant*.'"

Adams said he'd like some time to think about the idea. "All right," said Phillips, "you think about it. This is Saturday. You've got till Monday to make up your mind. That's when the Board meets.

"But I want you to know something else," Uncle Frank added. "Nobody else on the Board agrees with me that this is a good idea."

Adams recalls that all he could think of that weekend was that if he were to be Phillips' assistant, to be that close to him so much of the time, he would probably be sure to irritate him or alienate him. "Uncle Frank was a wonderful man, but the toughest task-master I have ever known. I figured that if I took the job, I didn't have a chance of staying with the company very long. But I also knew that if I *didn't* take it, I probably wouldn't be with the company even *that* long!"

"On Monday," Adams remembers, "Mr. Phillips called me in bright and early. He said, 'Young man, you've had enough time to think. Do you want the job or not?' I said, 'Mr. Phillips, you made up my mind last Saturday, but I didn't know it then. I'll take it.'"

During the first three weeks in his new post Adams was left strictly to himself; he did not get a single communication from Mr. Phillips. Then, on the Friday of the third week, Uncle Frank came into Adams' office and snapped, "Well, what have you been doing for the last three weeks?" Taking the bull by the horns, Adams calmly said he'd been making a list of the things he would do if he were president of the company. "This took even Uncle Frank back a little bit," Adams recalls. "I handed him the yellow sheets on which I'd made my notes, and he took them and walked out. That night, at home, I got a call from him summoning me to his house. He said he liked all the proposals except one—a suggestion for a budget

committee which, under the chairmanship of a company executive, would

ADAMS WAS ALWAYS AT UNCLE FRANK'S SIDE, *either on the court as a member of Phillips 66-ers basketball team, as shown in this charity benefit reunion of veterans of first team; or in the Board Room as a member of Phillips' Executive Committee.*

do long-range corporate financial planning. 'I'll approve the whole thing as it stands with this one exception,' Mr. Phillips said, and he gave me back the list with the name of the executive I'd suggested crossed out, and my name substituted as budget committee chairman."

From that time on—for 18 years, during which Adams was elected Executive Vice-President, President, and, upon Frank Phillips' retirement in 1949, Chief Executive Officer of the company—Boots worked with Uncle Frank seven days a week, often for as much as 18 or more hours a day. In all that time Adams never had a regular day off, never had a vacation, never knew at what time of day or night the summons would come to attend a meeting, to discuss a problem, to pack in ten minutes for a trip to the New York money markets or the southwestern oilfields. It was not unusual for Boots to take off in a company plane at 2 A.M. in order to be somewhere at 7 A.M. to inspect or to close a deal. (In the early days of aviation when night-flying was a risky affair, Phillips at one point forbade Adams to make any after-dark flights.)

*W*hen, in 1946, Adams married Dorothy Glynn Stephens, Phillips was reluctant to let him go on a honeymoon. "I recall Mr. Phillips saying, 'What are you going to do on your wedding trip?' and before I had a chance to reply he said, 'You can't be gone very long. I tell you what I'll do. You take that little Lockheed plane we've got and go on your honeymoon and be back in four or five days.' So I said fine and we flew out to California and took in the sights."

Even Uncle Frank, whose entire life was wrapped up in his company, and who felt that business did not only come before pleasure but *was* pleasure, admitted that Adams' assignment was vastly demanding. When Boots marked his 25th year with Phillips Petroleum, Uncle Frank wrote: "Not everyone is willing to assume the gruelling obligations imposed by executive assignments. Most people do not like to have business matters remain on their minds after going out of the office door at the end of a high pressure day. Nor do they like to be constantly aware of the responsibility involved in making quick decisions on matters of momentous consequences. Few persons relish a steady diet of troubles. [But Boots] does not allow difficulties to stand in the way of his going after anything that appears worthwhile; he works on the theory that anything can be accomplished if sufficient effort is put behind it."

WHEN BOOTS WED *his Texas-born bride, Dorothy Glynn Stephens, Uncle Frank offered him few days off for a honeymoon.*

In addition to the sheer demands of time and effort, Adams also had to cope with the hard-headedness and the quixotic temperament of his boss. "Frank Phillips was the toughest man I ever had to deal with," says Boots. "In the first place, he was a rugged individualist, and he wanted everyone who worked for him to know who was in charge." For example, in 1938, when Adams had just been elected President of the company, he concluded one of his major deals with a gas pipeline company. (Just four such Adams deals already have grossed Phillips Petroleum over $650,000,000.) The Board of Directors met in New York City to ratify it. Uncle Frank, then Chairman of the Board, opened the discussion on the resolution by announcing, "To start with, gentlemen, I'm against it." After Boots described the negotiations and arrangments in detail, Phillips called for a vote. Every director, knowing how Phillips felt about the deal, voted "nay." When it came Adams' turn to vote Phillips said, "You can't vote, Boots."

"You can't *keep* me from voting, Mr. Phillips," said Adams. "I'm a director, too."

Boots' vote was the only affirmative one. When the tally was officially complete, Uncle Frank smiled a slow smile. Then he shifted in his seat and said, "Now, gentlemen, it seems to me that we have a problem here. If we have a new President of this company, we really ought either to follow his recommendations, or to fire him. Let's take another vote on this proposal."

This time every director voted "aye" except Phillips himself— who abstained from voting!

As Adams points out today, "What Mr. Phillips was saying to me at the meeting was sparkling clear. He was saying: 'O.K., you do what you want to, what you think best; but remember, I'm still boss!'"

Adams often had to exert more ingenuity in convincing Phillips of the sagacity of a "deal" he had made for the company than he did to make the deal in the first place! For example, Boots maneuvered and negotiated for many years to establish Phillips as a major producer and transporter of natural gas. Uncle Frank, as was well known, was never truly convinced of the importance of natural gas. "Once, when I got back from an official closing on a gas acreage purchase," Adams remembers, "Mr. Phillips looked at me and said, 'Where've you been, out chasing

NEVER A LET-UP *in the work schedule. With Phillips and other executives, Adams works on field reports while flying to a meeting in Company plane. Far left is J.A. "Jim" Thompson, Boot's longtime secretary and aide; far right is John H. Kane, then V.P. and General Counsel.*

gas bubbles again?' And all I answered was, 'Yes, sir.' He never
said another word about it."

Another time, when Adams was working to get the company into
international areas of operation—a field long neglected because of Uncle
Frank's opposition to the idea—Boots succeeded in winning a promising oil
concession in the neutral zone between Kuwait and Saudi Arabia.
Proudly he reported to Mr. Phillips: "We're in the Middle East now!"
Replied Phillips: "I don't want to be in the Middle East!"
"But we're in it," said Adams. "I've been working for one year
and a half to *get* into it."
"Well," said Uncle Frank, "get out!"
Adams finally arranged a compromise plan whereby the concession
was turned into a cooperative venture with other oil companies under the
name of the American Independent Oil Co. It meant, in effect, that Phillips
had to yield two-thirds of its interest in the concession.

"Mr. Phillips fought me hard on many such deals," says Boots. "I think
he used to like to have me disagree with him because he was so prone to be
a bull in the woods, very dogmatic and opinionated. But he was always
completely fair. He'd often tell me I was a 'hard-headed Dutchman just like
your father, if you don't have your own way you're just not satisfied.'
But once I had convinced him that a certain deal was something we should
do, or if I had gone ahead and committed us to a position which
he couldn't countermand, he backed me all the way.
"After one particular deal involving a great amount of money, Uncle
Frank said to me: 'Boots, everybody thinks you're going to bankrupt the
company. So do I. But it's O.K. with me. We'll go into
bankruptcy together'."

The
"Play's"
The
Thing

ONE OF THE THINGS THAT HAS ALWAYS STAYED with Mrs. Luella Adams
was a remark her son made just before he went off to college.
"We were talking about the future," she recalled, "and Kenneth said to
me, 'You know, Mom, I'm not sure why or how, but I can just
see in my mind the plan for things.'"
All through his business career, Adams has demonstrated over and over
again this capacity he has for grasping concepts, for making decisions
based on what others might call "hunches"—in short, for "seeing the plan
for things." Men who have worked with him through the years
invariably comment on Boots' seeming sixth sense for opportunities,
and for the vigor with which he pursues them.
As we shall see, this ability of Adams' was eventually to be largely
responsible for the enormous success of Phillips Petroleum as a highly
diversified company. But the first concrete demonstration of Boots'
"nose" for deals came in the late 1920's and early 1930's, when the company
made its initial push to build up a distribution and marketing system—
including retail service stations—to sell its own products.

At first Phillips was solely an oil producer, selling its basic product
to other oil concerns that had refineries and distribution networks. But as
those other firms increased their own production of crude oil, and as
the automobile began to appear in increasing numbers on the nation's
spreading highway system, it became clear that to survive and prosper,
Phillips would have to refine and market its own output under
its own brand name. Forced to begin this move from a standing start, and
in the bleak Depression years, Phillips found the going tough.
After a discussion of the problem one day in Mr. Phillips' office, Adams
said: "Send me out, Mr. Phillips. I'll buy the sales outlets for you."
Less than a week later Adams went on the road carrying more than
one million dollars' worth of Phillips Petroleum Co. stock and bonds in a
small travel suitcase, assigned to acquire sales outlets that would
assure a continuing and dependable market for the company's products.
For months Boots crossed and re-crossed the country, putting in gruelling
20-hour days, locating properties, analyzing their potential, doing
everything from golfing with prospects to sympathizing with them about
their matrimonial problems. But he succeeded in putting together
a distribution network that enabled Phillips to compete on equal
terms in the industry.

FLYING FIELD SERVICE

ALWAYS FORWARD-LOOKING, *Adams encouraged Phillips to upgrade aviation gas, service planes with mobile airfield pump.*

WHEN ADAMS STARTED BUILDING UP
*network to market Phillips 66
name-brand products, opening of
new service station was
occasion for enthusiasm, color,
dramatic fanfare.*

Another famous example of Boots Adams' daring and foresight was the part he played in opening up the rich oil fields that lay underneath Oklahoma City, Okla. On March 26, 1930, a gusher known as the "Wild Mary Sudik" came in. Before it was controlled, it spouted 200 million cubic feet of gas and 20,000 barrels of oil a day—revealing the enormous untapped potential of the oil pool that ran beneath the city.
Phillips, along with other oil companies, leased acreage extending into the Oklahoma City limits. But the city zoning ordinances prohibited drilling for oil within much of the city limits. Although there was little question that huge oil reserves existed there, there was a serious question as to whether the local government would agree to modify the laws.
The nub of the matter was whether Phillips should lease more land within the city limits on the gamble that the zoning regulations would be changed in a popular election.

*A*dams, who had thoroughly discussed the situation with Robert R. Lynn, then Vice-President in charge of Land and Geology, told Frank Phillips that he thought that if a proposition to extend the oil-drilling area within the Oklahoma City limits could be put on the ballot, the people of the city would approve. Mr. Phillips had sent one of the company's senior officers to study the matter.
"I was sitting in on a meeting of our Executive Committee, not as a member but as Mr. Phillips' assistant," Adams recalls, "when this officer reported that the zoning extension wouldn't stand a chance of approval. Another objection was that we'd have to drill in heavily built-up city areas. Mr. Phillips listened, nodded, and said, 'Well, that's that. We're just not interested in Oklahoma City.' Then, before he closed the meeting, he turned to me and said, 'Well, now, Boots, what do you think about it?' I said, 'I don't agree at all. I'm sure the extension can be won.'
"That provoked Mr. Phillips a good bit. 'All right,' he said, 'if that's the way you feel, you go down there and do something about it.'"
That same evening Adams gathered a group of young Phillips experts, went to Oklahoma City, and within a few days had put together an organization of about 50 men. Working day and night, they spent millions of dollars buying up leases on land within the city limits. As Bob Lynn says, "Oklahoma City was a rough-tough play . . . a lot tougher than most people knew. For one thing, each block within the city limits had about

30 or 40 lots on it. You had to buy leases on each individual lot, and get 51% of the owners on a block to agree to the drilling of one well on each block. The prices would go higher every day. Then, *if* we won the election and *did* drill, we would have to buy a couple of houses on each block, jack them up and move them away in order to clear an area for the derrick. This play would mean risking an awful lot of money."

On top of everything else, there was a ticklish local political situation. Some independent oil men, powerful in city affairs, owned leases that benefited from oil drainage from the areas inside the city limits. If the zoning were changed and drilling extended within that area of the city, the drainage might be lost to them. This made for a great deal of hard in-fighting.

*J*ust how hard is evidenced by one anecdote Adams tells. "I remember one night I was called by an oil man. As I walked into his hotel room he pointedly placed a gun on the table. He asked me if I was going to keep on fighting for the zoning extension. I said yes. 'I'm going to fight you,' he said, sort of running his hand along the gun. 'You just go ahead and fight us,' I said. 'That's what I'm going to do,' he replied, 'I just wanted to tell you that.' Having that gun out there was impressive, but I wasn't really disturbed about it. Maybe he thought it would have some influence on me."

Adams was in Oklahoma City for the better part of six months, supervising the leasing of lots; running a special daily newspaper that campaigned for the zoning extension; contacting everyone and anyone he thought might help. One of the men whose aid Adams enlisted was an oil driller named Robert Kerr. Adams got Kerr to take the leadership of the Adams-formed Oklahoma City Extension Association, and Kerr's activity in that campaign was the start of his public career that led to his eventually becoming Governor of the State and U. S. Senator.

According to Clarence O. Stark, former Vice President for Land and Geology, "the only reason that campaign ever got won was because of Boots himself. He had the ability to pick the right people to handle the job in Oklahoma City, and he himself was on duty almost all the time. I used to say to him, 'While those other guys are sleeping, you're down here working.' When he faced a problem he'd talk to ten people, digest what they told him, and then come up with an answer—usually the right one."

AFTER ADAMS WON UPHILL FIGHT *for right to drill within new areas of Oklahoma City, rigs burgeoned around State Capitol grounds.*

BOOTS' ENTHUSIASTIC FORESIGHT *on the potential of natural gas and its liquids led to the construction of such pioneering plants to process the "gas bubbles."*

The vote was close, but the proposal to change the zoning laws to permit the extension of drilling inside the city limits was approved. As soon as the returns were in Adams had his work-crews ready to go, setting up equipment and starting to drill.

The Oklahoma City wells, still producing today, have been among the most prolific and profitable wells in the U. S. Because Adams "stuck his neck out and succeeded," as Dean McGee, head of the Kerr-McGee Oil Co. says, Phillips Petroleum walked off with a major share of this rich field. It was one of the big strides in the company's march toward becoming a giant of the industry.

*W*hen veterans of Phillips get together, the talk usually gets around to some of the other famous "plays" that developed as a result of Boots Adams' willingness to gamble on his hunches. For instance, despite promising geologic reports on a huge acreage of Gulf Coast land known as the Chocolate Bayou field, the first two test wells drilled there turned out to be dry holes. "Where shall we drill next?" someone asked. Adams said, "Let's try half a mile south." They did—and brought in a gusher, the first of many in that field!

Another time Adams was flying over the Texas Gulf coast, near Corpus Christi, with Bob Lynn. As they passed over Copano Bay, Boots glanced down and saw a single drilling rig in the water. "That looks like something we ought to buy," he said to Lynn; and on virtually no other basis than that, Phillips did buy the acreage—which turned out to be a bonanza.

But the talk also reveals that the Adams' hunches were not always quite so "iffy" as they may have seemed. True, Adams did "like the looks" of the Copano Bay play. But according to Clarence Stark, "Adams went around talking to all the people he could get hold of who knew anything at all about the area. He just listened and listened and found out all the information he could. It was not till after he'd done this groundwork that we doubled, tripled, and even quadrupled the 'play.' When we finally got around to drilling, we opened up a major oil and gas field."

In another "play"—the highly productive and profitable West Edmond Field, north of Oklahoma City—Adams went directly against the advice of most of the experts in his Land and Geology Department.

58

ANGLE PICTURE *dramatizes grace and power of Phillips rig drilling world's deepest hole, five miles down.*

Boots tells the story this way:

"In the early thirties there was a small airport right at the edge of what is now the West Edmond Field where I often landed. It was just an asphalt airstrip on a knoll. Every time I got out of the plane I used to say, 'I think we're right on top of a structure here.' I didn't know a damned thing about geology, but it looked to me like we were on top of oil. I guess I talked about it so many times I finally convinced myself there was oil there."

Several years later an independent operator sank a well in the area. When Adams learned the well had had a show of oil, he became convinced all over again that West Edmond was on top of a major oil field. He sent a land crew to the region with orders to buy acreage. After a few weeks the crew manager called Adams and said, "I want to come home and talk to you about this play."

"You stay down there," replied Adams. "You keep buying acreage. I sent you down, and I'll tell you when to come home."

Two weeks later Adams got another call from his man. "I've spent $1,500,000, and I'm coming home to talk to you."

What worried the Phillips geologists was that the entire West Edmond play was in a "tight" formation known as Hunton Lime. This is a low-porosity limestone stratum in which the oil is tightly locked. In order to force the oil to flow freely enough to make a well productive, acid had to be pumped into the Hunton Lime to "eat out" channels in the rock. Adams was told by his experts that the play would never make the company any money: that the combination of well-depth and the need for acid would be too costly.

"Why didn't I pay any attention to the geologists?" says Adams. "Because I was convinced we were on top of a major field. I believed in the acid, I believed in the play."

Or, as Boots had years earlier said to his mother, "I can see in my mind the plan for things."

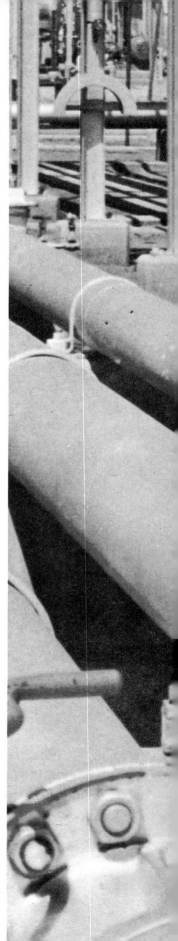

O<small>N</small> J<small>UNE</small> 13, 1935, <small>A LETTER REACHED BOOTS ADAMS' DESK</small> that was to prove historic in the development of Phillips Petroleum Co. It was from George G. Oberfell, then Vice-President of the Research and Development Department. Across the top were these words: "A Dry Gas Well is an Oil Well."

Today this may seem like an obvious statement. But in the days when Oberfell said it, most oilmen considered natural gas not only worthless, but a nuisance. True, its pressure helped to force oil to the surface; but whereas oil could be barreled and transported to markets, the business of piping gas over long distances was then in its infancy. The result was that trillions of cubic feet of natural gas were being flared off as waste.

Phillips, which had long since become a major user and supplier of motor fuel components physically separated from natural gas, had been experimenting in a comparatively limited way with chemical methods of converting the liquids found in natural gas products which could be blended with oil-refinery gasoline to produce a superior motor fuel. But the idea of building up large natural-gas reserves was consistently thumbed down by Frank Phillips. When Oberfell's letter reached Adams, however, it fell upon more fertile ground. The letter read:

> *"Dear Sir:*
> *"At present we are actually making, at a lower cost, just as much motor fuel from a 25 million cubic foot gas well in the Panhandle as from a 300 barrel oil well. In a few years we should be making just as much motor fuel from a 25 million cubic foot gas well as from a 500 barrel oil well. It is not unreasonable to expect that in less than ten years time the 25 million cubic foot gas well will be equal to a 1,000 barrel oil well, or perhaps eventually a 2,000 barrel oil well, as far as motor fuel production is concerned.*
> *"The above statement is offered merely as a means of emphasizing the tremendous potential importance to Phillips Petroleum Company of gas reserves ..."*

Says Adams, "This letter so impressed me about the real potential value of gas that I kept it for years in my desk and used it as my Bible. And it gave me the germ of the idea of how necessary it was for Phillips to have substantial gas reserves at a time when you could get gas acreage for practically nothing because gas was considered a waste product. Mr. Phillips did not agree with me, but he didn't order me *not* to buy any."

62

<small>AT ONE OF MORE THAN 50</small> *Phillips gas processing plants, natural gas is separated from its liquids which include natural gasoline and liquefied petroleum gases.*

WORKMAN SURVEYS MAZE *of pipes, stacks, storage tanks*
at a major Phillips crude oil and natural gas liquids processing center near Borger, Texas.

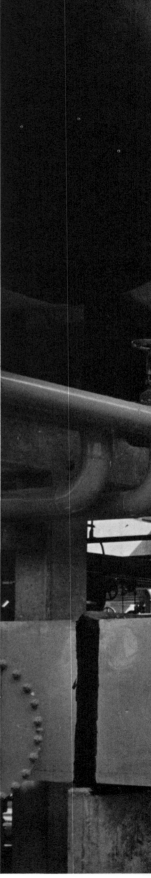

The long years of stoking a coal furnace, first at home and then in his fraternity house, gave Boots another reason to envision how cheap, clean, easy-to-handle gas for heating would virtually sell itself. "I could see the ultimate industrial and home heating demand for gas if it could be piped economically from the fields to distributing centers," says Adams. So he began a long-term program of buying natural gas acreage, and buying and building trans-continental pipeline systems.

The fantastic growth of the nation's gas pipeline system in the 1940's made gas eagerly sought after. Adams' gamble—plus his persistence—began to pay off. In addition, it was this foresight of Adams that continued Phillips' position as the world's largest producer of natural gas liquids and in turn, as we shall see, to its top ranking in the field of petrochemicals.

Two of Adams' most astute and important natural gas purchases were the Hugoton acreage in the Texas-Oklahoma Panhandle, and the Shamrock properties in Texas. Some Phillips veterans claim that the Hugoton purchase has earned more money for the company than any other single deal. It had its inception (as did so many others) as a result of Boots' many close friendships with people in the oil industry. This particular friend, faced with the need to raise a substantial amount of money, had to sell 341,000 proven acres. Bargaining started at an asking price of $25 an acre, but Adams would go no higher than $10. Eventually, on the day after Christmas, the owner came to Adams, threw a briefcase full of land maps on Adams' desk, and said, "O.K., they're yours. But I've got to have the money by December 31."

Delighted, Adams went to tell Mr. Phillips the good news. But Phillips said, "Now, Boots, you know I'm not buying any gas acreage." One valid point that Uncle Frank made was that the purchase, for all cash, would at the time have depleted the company's cash position. But so persuasive was the Adams' tongue that Phillips not only went along with the deal, but proudly put up $1,000,000 of his own money, at a nominal one per cent interest, to make it feasible.

The Shamrock gas acreage purchase took more than four years to mature. In the early stages of negotiations, Frank Phillips reiterated his objections to "getting in the gas business" on the grounds that what natural gas wasn't being flared away in the air was being sold for one cent

66

SWEENY REFINERY, *on Texas Gulf Coast, part of Adams' product upgrading program, is also key center for processing natural gas liquids and manufacturing petrochemicals.*

per thousand cubic feet. Twice Adams had to cancel purchase contracts before Mr. Phillips finally approved the third deal.

The gas pipeline from the Texas Panhandle to Michigan and Wisconsin was another of Adams' brain-children. When Federal Government regulations prevented Phillips Petroleum from building its own pipeline on that route, Adams worked out a plan with William Woolfolk, President of the Michigan Consolidated Gas Company, whereby that concern would organize the Michigan-Wisconsin Pipeline Company to build and maintain the pipeline, and Phillips would furnish all the natural gas. The deal was to be consummated in New York, in Mr. Woolfolk's offices on Broadway. But just before the papers were to be signed, the "welcome-home" parade for General Eisenhower, who had returned from Europe as the victorious World War II Commander-in-Chief, started up the traditional Broadway route.

"I'll never forget," says Boots, "I was leaning out the window, trying to see through the flying confetti and paper streamers, when Mr. Woolfolk suddenly ran over and pulled me back from the ledge. 'My God,' he said, 'I thought you were going to fall out that window and there would go my pipeline.' I said, 'Well, I won't lean out quite so far but I've just got to see General Eisenhower.' I started to lean out again when suddenly Mr. Woolfolk just slammed that window down. He didn't want to run *any* risks!"

*B*ut the long-range effects of Adams' knowledgeable insistence on getting into natural gas early were far more important than immediate profits. Boots' determination to "chase gas bubbles" has made Phillips the top American handler of natural gas; the leading producer and distributor of such liquefied petroleum gases as butane and propane; and one of the most diversified of present-day oil companies. For the move into natural gas led Phillips, by a series of intermediate steps, into the basic research program which gave it such a headstart in the development of its far-flung petrochemical complexes.

Early in 1925 Phillips Petroleum was sued for alleged patent infringement by a major chemical corporation in connection with its technique for separating the components of natural gasoline, now more commonly called natural gas liquids. To defend the suit, the company employed some researchers. When the suit was won by Phillips, it was decided to continue

SNOW AND FIR TREES *as background for machinery, symbolize Adams' move in Canadian oil country.*

KANSAS CITY REFINERY *which produces quality lubricants and high-octane motor fuels, glows with night-time brilliance.*

their activities and organize a broadly-based Research Department.
As a result, today only twelve industrial companies hold more U. S. patents
than Phillips does. And among oil companies, only giant Standard
of New Jersey outranks it in this regard.

The key to these efforts is Boots Adams' basic business principle:
up-grading. That has become a familiar word at Phillips—and what it
means is using brains and skill and drive to get the last scrap of value out
of every enterprise. Thus, from a pound of crude liquid hydrocarbons
worth, say, one cent, Phillips could produce an amount of gasoline worth
about two cents. But the same materials, if up-graded through chemical
processes, could be turned into products worth five or ten times as much.
For example, as natural gas is stripped of certain of its constituent
hydrocarbon molecules, the basic raw material can be made to yield not
only natural gasoline and LP gases, but also the chemical building blocks for
such end-products as synthetic fibers; nitrogen fertilizers; aerosol
propellants; polyethylene plastics which can be used in items ranging from
ski-tow ropes and industrial mouldings to consumer packaging; and,
from the butadiene in natural gas, synthetic rubber for tires.

*T*he story of Phillips' entry into the field of synthetic rubber reflects
Boots Adams' up-grading process at work in both oil and natural gas.
According to George G. Oberfell, Adams questioned him about the
advisability of doing research on natural-gas derived carbon black, a
substance that adds toughness and mileage to tires, sometime about the
beginning of the 1940's. "I explained to him" said Oberfell, "that
we didn't make carbon black ourselves, but merely sold the natural gas to
carbon black manufacturers, because we were so involved in research
problems on other products which seemed to have priority. Adams said,
'You are probably right,' and seemed to dismiss the matter from his mind."

But as oilmen know, Adams seldom entirely dismisses any matter from
his mind. For if carbon black could be made from oil, it would be cheaper
than that made from gas. Also, its characteristics could be varied to make
it usable in many different kinds of rubber. Six months later Adams
called Oberfell to his office and said, "I've decided to build a plant to make
carbon black out of oil instead of gas. So you'd better get a research
program started on it right away." Typically, it wasn't long before
Oberfell's staff came up with a way of manufacturing carbon black from

72

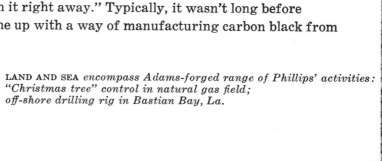

LAND AND SEA *encompass Adams-forged range of Phillips' activities:
"Christmas tree" control in natural gas field;
off-shore drilling rig in Bastian Bay, La.*

AGLEAM IN THE NIGHT, *ammonia plant at Adams Terminal, takes on a fairyland aspect.*

oil, rather than gas. The break-through proved to be a major contribution to the quality of synthetic rubber; and Phillips was for some time the only company with the know-how needed to build and operate the new process.

Adams' move into synthetic rubber marked Phillips' first step in its program of petrochemical diversification. And the way the move developed is another typical "Boots" adventure in combining foresight, negotiating skill, and gambling nerve.

*I*n 1942, when it became apparent that the full-scale development of synthetic rubber would be important to the nation's war effort, the Federal Government was prepared to call on private industry in building a synthetic rubber plant. Adams went to Washington to negotiate with Jesse Jones, then head of the Reconstruction Finance Corporation. At stake was RFC approval for the construction and operation of a $38,000,000 plant at Borger, Texas, by Phillips, drawing on its natural gas resources for raw materials. Adams clinched the delicate deal with a characteristic maneuver: making seemingly complex financial calculations on a slide-rule when, in actuality, he had no idea at all of how a slide-rule worked!

Shortly afterwards, Frank Phillips went to Washington. During a visit to his old friend Jesse Jones, Mr. Phillips got into a violent argument with the RFC administrator. The result was a curt wire from Jones to Adams cancelling the government contract for Phillips Petroleum to build the plant. When Boots agonizedly confronted Mr. Phillips with the telegram, the latter said, "Well, at least we're out of the rubber business." But Adams, moving full speed ahead as usual, had already committed between three and four million dollars in land, supplies and other preliminary arrangements for the Borger factory. Without the RFC contract, that money and effort would go down the drain.

"I went back to Washington," Adams recalls, "to try to dream up a way to reinstate the contract. By talking in a seemingly casual way with several influential people, I managed to plant the idea that it would provoke quite a scandal if it should be learned that the government was not pressing its synthetic-rubber effort."

It didn't take long, in war-time Washington, for the word to get out that the whole synthetic-rubber program was to be investigated by a U. S. Senate Committee, headed by a Senator named Harry Truman, and that Boots Adams was scheduled to be the first witness.

ADAMS' BRAIN CHILDREN.
Above is part of world's largest carbon black plant at Borger, Texas, producing an essential component for the creation of synthetic rubber used for modern tires. Below is multi-tentacled pipeline complex at Phillips' East St. Louis, Ill. terminal.

With this gossip spreading through the capital's grapevine, Adams went
to see Jesse Jones. "I told him" says Adams, "that not only was it not fair
for him to cancel our contract, but that there was to be a big flap
over the whole rubber shortage, and that I was going to be the first witness.
Jones was chary at first. 'Where'd you hear that?' he asked me.
Just then he got a note from his secretary summoning him to a high-level
meeting to discuss the rubber question. Jones looked at the note, and
then at me, and said: 'My God, Boots, you're right!'
"As Jones got ready to go to the meeting, I said, 'Shall I call you later?'
Jones said, 'You sit right where you are and wait till I get back!'"
Later that afternoon Jones and Adams were deep in re-negotiating their
arrangements. Boots, meanwhile, had been avoiding all calls from
Mr. Phillips, who still wanted to "stay out of rubber." But when the
arrangements were completed, Adams felt it should be cleared with him.
"I finally reached Mr. Phillips at his optometrist's," Boots remembers.
"I told him what I thought was the good news. Mr. Phillips said,
'Damn it, my eyes are dilated and I can't see a thing, and I don't want to
make that deal!' With that, he hung up on me. I turned to Jesse Jones and
said, "Mr. Phillips says he is very pleased we could work this out."
When Adams returned to Bartlesville with the contract for the Borger
plant and presented it to the Executive Committee for approval,
Mr. Phillips maintained an icy reserve on the matter. After it won an
affirmative vote Phillips said to Adams: "You like Washington so much
I ought to get you in the Army and send you there to fight the war."
"I'd much rather stay in Bartlesville and fight this war with you,"
Adams replied.

*I*N 1958 BOOTS ADAMS TOOK A TRIP AROUND THE WORLD. The journey had its inception in an invitation from Robert Anderson, Secretary of the Treasury under President Eisenhower, for Adams to be one of his economic advisers at an International Monetary Association conference in New Delhi, India. Many men, perhaps, might have been content with the honor and the pleasure of the experience, and more or less simply "gone along for the ride."

But Adams, characteristically, used the opportunity to acquaint himself with the trend of business in general—and of the oil and petrochemical business in particular—in Europe, Africa and Asia. And what he saw and heard convinced him that it was time for Phillips to get its feet wet in international oil operations. Up to that point, the company's only overseas operations were confined to a relatively small field in Venezuela and in the joint venture in the Kuwait neutral zone.

"In every city and country we visited on the trip," Adams says, "I had a chance to get to speak with local business and financial leaders. These were invaluable contacts in terms of getting economic information, and in terms of exploring what specific projects Phillips might get underway in these countries.

"I became convinced Europe was on the threshold of an industrial boom and an economic expansion, and I felt that Phillips would have to set up an international department as quickly as possible to expand its oil, gas and chemical business in as many countries as it could. It seemed to me we had only five to ten years to do the job, if we were going to be able to compete successfully with companies that were already in the international field."

The success of Adams' planning is evidenced by this roll-call of countries in which Phillips now has exploration, production, manufacturing, and sales enterprises underway:

In Libya and Algeria, oil has been found in large concessions, and is starting to flow to the seaports through newly-built pipelines. New oil reserves have been discovered in Venezuela. In Australia, a potentially substantial natural gas field has been found. Exploration for oil and gas is going on in many additional areas including the Gulf of Papua, the North Sea, the United Arab Republic, offshore Iran, Nigeria, and Colombia. Refining interests are in Canada, Venezuela, Great Britain, Kuwait and India. Phillips 66 service stations are in Venezuela and

80

ADAMS' ENERGY NEVER LAGS *despite his many duties:*
presiding at a Company annual meeting;
opening a new Phillips facility;
going to Japan to talk with leading industrialist;
or conferring with Prince Izzatt Gaafer of Saudi Arabia.

LIFE IS ALWAYS *rich and full for Boots.*
He may be identifying a Phillips 66-er player
for an announcer at a basketball game,
taking part in festivities
opening a Phillips service station,
or shaking many hands in reception line
at a Company function. But he still finds time
to unwind and relax at home with his wife.

Australia. LP-gas marketing is spreading rapidly to many countries. Petrochemical facilities abroad—partly or wholly owned by Phillips—include plants functioning or being built for the production of synthetic rubber, carbon black, butadiene, plastics, and other products. The company's petrochemical interests are in such countries as Spain, Belgium, Australia, Mexico, Colombia, Japan, South Africa, and India.

As Adams points out, expansion overseas is not merely a matter of looking for new oil or gas fields. "It is also a matter," he says, "of building plants and setting up marketing organizations. You might say we are trying to establish a small Phillips Petroleum Company in each of the countries we are going into. We are building up our reserves of raw material, establishing pipeline and distribution networks, and developing our petrochemical business—all at the same time.

"If you were going to choose a word to characterize the state of our international development now, the word would be 'preliminary.' We're still putting many more millions of dollars a year into our international expansion program than we're taking out. But it is beginning to pay off."

Among the personal reminiscences of his global journey, Adams likes to remember bargaining with merchants in the bazaars of India and Turkey; getting his hair cut by a "floating barber" while he was spending a week on a houseboat on a lake in the Vale of Kashmir; and deciding to go into the custom tailoring business in Hong Kong.

The latter was an expensive lesson. Impressed by the amount of business Chinese tailors did with tourists in Hong Kong, Adams and one of his traveling companions organized the Hong Kong Tailoring Company, which grew to three floors where Chinese tailors operated more than one thousand sewing machines.

"But after about four years we had to close up shop," says Boots. "I think I lost about $250,000 in that venture, so that visit of four or five days in Hong Kong turned out to be quite an expensive sojourn." Temporarily cautious, as a result, about doing business in the unfathomable Orient, Adams turned down an opportunity to take an interest in building a new hotel in Hong Kong. But unlike the tailoring company, the hotel turned out to be a phenomenal success.

Says Adams ruefully: "I missed the boat on that one."

As Boots Sees Others: The Philosophy of Leadership

*I*F YOU TALK FOR A WHILE WITH A PHILLIPS MAN—be he a key management executive or a rank-and-file employee—the chances are you'll be told a story something like these:

"There was a natural gas play up in the San Juan Basin, at the 'Four Corners' where Colorado, New Mexico, Arizona, and Utah meet. We looked it over and got all the information, and it shaped up as one of those deals where you might make a lot of money, and on the other hand you might not. But we figured we ought to risk it. Boots asked us how much money we'd need to make the gamble, and we said about two million dollars. Boots thought it over for about ten seconds. Then he said, 'Okay, you've got it.'"

"I left Bartlesville around 5 o'clock on a Friday night to bid on an oil lease near Ada, Oklahoma. By 10 the next morning I'd bought it for $1,150,000. I got to Bartlesville that afternoon to get the approval of the management. Mr. Phillips was out of town, and when the men on the Executive Committee heard what I'd done they all got up and left the meeting room, except for Boots. At that time Boots was still just Mr. Phillips' assistant. But he had the guts to say, 'Well, if no one objects— and there doesn't seem to be anybody left here *to* object—I say let's approve this.' It shows how Boots would stick by his people. He wouldn't let you down when you stuck your neck out."

"I was sent out to buy service stations and arrange to have bulk storage plants built in the days when Phillips was on a crash program to build up its own marketing network. I'd been gone five days when I got a call from Boots. 'How many stations have you bought?' he asked. I said, 'None, yet.' Then he said, 'How many bulk plants have you built?' I said, 'Well, sir, none.' Then he said, 'I think you better come home for a little talk,' and I figured I was going to get fired. But Boots put his arm around my shoulders. 'Look, I know that in the job you had before, you couldn't do anything without sending in memos and reporting to committees and getting everything approved. But Phillips is different. If you see something you want to buy, go ahead and buy it. If you want to build a bulk plant, go ahead and build it. Just keep wiring home for money.'"

In 1946, in a report to stockholders at the annual Phillips meeting, Frank Phillips said: "The most valued possession that we have is the human organization which mans all our assignments." That is even more true today. Security analysts and business reporters—notoriously hard-headed people —invariably make a point of employee loyalty when writing about Phillips.

86

BOOTS IS AS POPULAR *at play as at work.*
At a Woolaroc Ranch barbecue for the Jesters,
social organization of the Masonic Shrine,
his autograph is eagerly sought.

Perhaps one of the major factors in the growth of this loyalty has been Boots Adams' handling of people: his confidence in their ability, his willingness to gamble on their know-how, his readiness to give them quick decisions, his loyalty in backing up subordinates. All of this is part not only of Adams' own character, but of his philosophy of leadership. "I can think of no single thing," Adams once said, "so essential to the welfare of our company as a reservoir of human energy, resourcefulness and ingenuity."

Despite the fact that Adams was the "man in charge" for so many years, Phillips is not a one-man company. "Each man in our top executive team can run the show, and sometimes does when the rest of them are away," says Adams. The present team—Vice-Chairman Paul Endacott, President Stanley Learned, Executive Committee Chairman William W. Keeler, and Executive Vice-President John M. Houchin—is used to huddling quickly to make quick decisions.

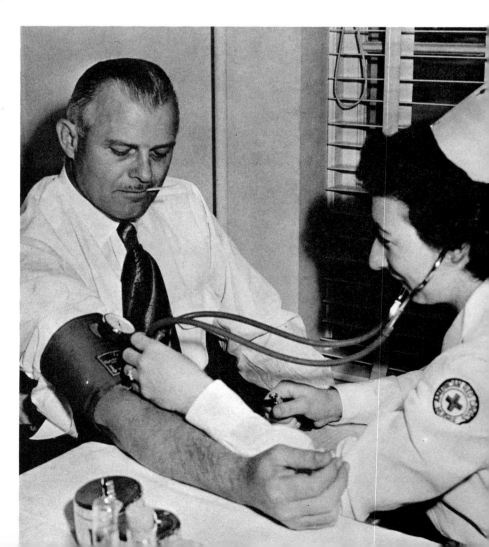

GREGARIOUS AND CIVIC-MINDED, *Adams gives of his time to many activities:*
at Jester fund-raising gathering;
donating to Red Cross Blood Bank;
chatting informally with attendant at Pier 66 Marina, Fort Lauderdale, Fla.

AT EASE WITH ALL COMERS,
*Adams swaps yarns
with the hands on
bunkhouse porch at his
Foraker, Okla. ranch.*

A second point is Adams' adherence to the principle of trusting the competence and judgment of the men he hires and promotes. He has often told his executives: "Each of you has the ability to say 'Yes' on anything you want to do. I'm the only one who can say 'No.'"

As Adams observed recently, "That's one of the ways we've built this company. For example, one of our key men came to me some years ago to tell me Phillips had been offered an opportunity to bid on the purchase of a Gulf Coast refinery, but that he had turned it down because Phillips wasn't interested in having a refinery on the Gulf Coast. I said, 'You had all the authority in the world to go ahead and bid on the property. But you had no authority to say we weren't interested.'

"We made that deal," Adams continued, "and it was the start of our Sweeny Refinery—a project which has grossed over two-and-a-half billion dollars for the company so far. A man must be willing to chance saying 'yes' rather than 'no.' A man must make mistakes; if he doesn't, he isn't doing anything. He's like the baseball player who seldom makes an error because he doesn't try for the hard plays."

A third aspect of Adams' philosophy of leadership is accessibility. His door is always open to anyone in the company. "Why not?" says gregarious Boots. "I like people, all kinds of people. I like to talk to them. And one never knows where the next good idea is going to come from."

What kind of qualities in people does Adams look for most?

"To me, the main point is creative ability," he says. "What's important is whether a man can create something from his own thinking that will become tangible—whether he can come up with an idea that can be firmed up into a deal or a project. I look for a man who can judge what *ought* to be done that is *not now* being done. A man who has two good creative ideas out of five, he's on the plus side all the time.

"A lot of creative men are rabbit chasers. They have ideas and can work on deals but never close one. To be successful, once a man gets an idea and is convinced of it, he must make it an actuality. And he's got to know he has the authority to go out and close a deal. You can have a lot of good ideas, but if you can't ever bring them to a conclusion you are just spinning your wheels and wasting your company's time.

"The fellow who has the idea in the first place, and has the thinking to

BOOTS ENJOYS MEETING ALL PEOPLE:
Mrs. Dwight D. Eisenhower and a young nephrosis victim,
as part of a charity appeal;
a shirt-sleeved co-worker;
or as the dedication speaker
at a new high school in Borger, Texas.

HOWDY BOOTS

bring it to real life—he's the man to put your money on. We built Phillips Petroleum Company in Bartlesville, a small town in the Midwest. Nobody ever comes here to give you any ideas. You have to create them yourself."

Some years ago Adams formulated his philosophy of what makes for business success in a talk to Phillips executives. These are the points he listed:

DETERMINATION—*"a burning desire to succeed ... a willingness to make any and all personal sacrifices of time and talents to accomplish this objective ... this drive manifests itself in highly concentrated energy determined to accomplish all assignments—challenging or routine, pleasant or unpleasant—as speedily and efficiently as possible."*

LEADERSHIP—*"an ability to get along with people ... consideration for the feelings of others ... a man who is liked as an individual, respected as a leader, who is just with criticism and quick with praise."*

SELF-CONFIDENCE—*"an assurance in his own ability and judgment, a willingness to make decisions because he is sure of what he is doing ... he profits by mistakes rather than letting the consequence of his errors shatter his confidence."*

ANALYTICAL ABILITY—*"the type of mind that recognizes essentials and refuses to be distracted by non-essentials. He refuses to be influenced solely by the obvious but searches out less relevant details that bear on the ultimate decision."*

ORIGINALITY—*"This man goes on the assumption that improvement is always possible ... limitations do not exist for him ... by initiative and imagination he enlarges the scope of his functions ... he is quick to recognize the value of new ideas from others, and encourage their development."*

SELF-EXPRESSION—*"the ability to use the right words at the right time."*

LOYALTY—*"a deep faith that the organization of which he is a part is performing a worthwhile service that deserves his wholehearted effort ..."*

If one reviews that list and matches it against Adams' own demands upon himself during *his* business career, it seems clear that his philosophy of leadership is no textbook sort of affair, but one drawn from the principles that have actuated his own life.

As Others See Him: The Many Faces of Boots

ON THE 18TH FLOOR OF THE NEW PHILLIPS BUILDING in Bartlesville, teak-panelled reception rooms lead into the private office of Boots Adams. Save for an ashtray and cigarette box, a pen set and a calendar clock, the massive desk is uncluttered. Even the telephone is hidden inside a special drawer. The room is brightened with photographs of Adams' friends and family; with mementoes, notably a Presidential seal inscribed, *"To K. S. Adams with grateful appreciation, Dwight D. Eisenhower, 1956";* with a framed cartoon of a board of directors' meeting with the gagline: *"Besides investing, merging and expanding, does anyone know how we can make a few bucks?"* In the office there are two portraits of Adams by his friend and golfing partner, President Eisenhower, one formal and one of Adams as a golfer. Eisenhower wrote to him: "I hope you were not too shocked when you got a chance to look at my poor efforts to capture your likeness. The photographs from which I had to work showed your teeth. I did not want to attempt a painting of teeth. I had to paint that part of your face with imagination."

This is, indeed, the sanctum of a business leader. And because for so many years Adams has been the public embodiment of a major corporation, there is a tendency to think of him only as an industrial executive. But

PORTRAIT OF GOLFER ADAMS *was painted by good friend, Dwight D. Eisenhower, as was formal portrait on the preceding page.*

BOOTS GETS WELCOME HANDSHAKE *from*
another good friend, President Lyndon B. Johnson.

with best wishes,
Lyndon B. Johnson

there are, of course, many other faces of Boots Adams—many ways in which different people see him, and know him.

As a husband and father, and son and brother, Adams is a devoted family man. In 1945, on a business trip to San Antonio, Texas, he met Dorothy Glynn Stephens, the sister-in-law of a geophysicist who was doing work for Phillips.

"After we got through talking business," Boots remembers, "I talked to her about going out for something to eat, or for the evening. She said, fine. And it got to where about every weekend I wanted to go to San Antonio, and Mr. Phillips said to me one day, 'What are you doing in San Antonio so often? If you've got a girl friend down there, you bring her up here, because I want to meet her.' So I brought her up here and showed her off, and a little over a year later we got married."

*T*he Adamses have five children: Stephen Stanley, 17; Kenneth Glenn, 16; Gary Clark, 14; Stephanie Lyn, 12; and Lisa Ann, 10. (Adams' older children by a previous marriage are Kenneth S. Adams, Jr., a Houston, Texas, industrialist and owner of the Houston Oilers football team; and Mary Louise (Mrs. John) Hendricks, of Shreveport, La.)

As a family man, Boots takes his responsibilities seriously. He and his wife have taken pains to bring their children up with discipline. Says Adams: "Dorothy Glynn's a wonderful mother. She works day and night on our children. She really raises them!" Despite the demands of business, Adams has made it a point to share in as many of their activities as possible. He is a familiar figure at PTA meetings, Boy Scout meetings, school athletic events, Sunday worship at the First Presbyterian Church. "It's hard to fit all this into a busy schedule, but I've just made up my mind to do it," Adams says. "It keeps you hopping, but it also keeps you young. As Mr. Phillips once said to me, 'By having youth around you, you stay young yourself.'"

In addition to his family responsibilities, Adams has also been a dynamic worker for his community and state. He has been a Commander of the Bartlesville American Legion Post, President of its Chamber of Commerce, and officer of countless civic and fraternal organizations. Behind the scenes he has given widely of his time and energy to many civic and charitable projects in both Bartlesville and Oklahoma.

Another face of Boots is Adams the farmer-rancher. His mother remembers that young Kenneth used to spend boyhood summers at his grandfather's

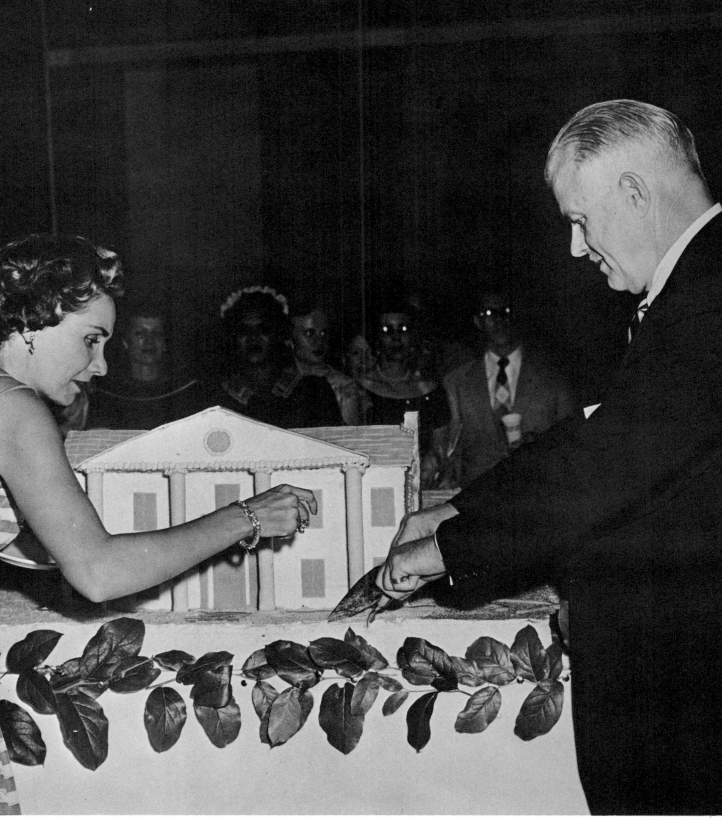

CELEBRATING *his 55th birthday Boots, with his wife's assistance, cuts huge cake given by co-workers.*

farm in Horton, Kansas. "He'd follow his grandpa around and watch him
with horses and cattle," she said. "Kenneth got his love of animals,
I think, from this."

On his 1,500-acre Ken-Ada farm home, which he can see from his office
windows, Adams for many years ran a registered Holstein dairyfarm
operation. When a combination of low milk prices and high feed prices
made this impractical, he switched to Angus beef cattle. Most of Adams'
important agricultural work, however, goes on at his 33,000-acre
ranch at Foraker, Okla., which is widely known for its successful
experimentation in livestock production—Whiteface, Hereford and Black
Angus cattle—and in land management. Under the direction of a top
agronomist, the farm has tested grasses, sods and plants. His support of
land management experiments has won Adams honors from the
American Range Management Association.

Adams seldom takes time off for sheer relaxation. Friends point out that
even when he and his family are at their lake retreat at Grand Lake,
Okla., he will spend much of the day on the telephone while everyone else
is swimming or fishing. (Sometimes Boots will try to clear up most
of his business calls via the mobile radio-telephone in his car, so that when
he gets home he will not be called away from his family.) But even
when he does go on vacation his eye is still on the lookout for business
possibilities. For example, the Adams family spent some holiday time, some
years ago, in Fort Lauderdale, Fla. While there, Boots learned about
a new highway that was to be cut through an area that was then mostly
marshland. He bought land for Phillips with the idea that it could be turned
into a marina which would sell Phillips marine gasoline, and also serve
as an institutional advertisement for the company. Today Pier 66, as the
complex is called, is one of the East Coast's best-known and busiest
marinas. Under construction there is a 17-story hotel (to be Florida's
tallest hotel) with a revolving penthouse cocktail lounge.

When Adams does get away from his desk and phone it is usually on a
hunting or fishing trip (though, again, often with business associates).
Each year he takes his sons to New Mexico for a deer or elk hunt.
The practical joker in Boots finds its outlet on these jaunts. Arthur Hughes,
a former Phillips Vice-President, tells about the time he "shot my barrel
hot" and failed to hit one bird during a day of pheasant hunting. "Now, I

A COUNTRY BOY AT HEART, *Boots tends to ranch duties such as inspecting bulls in his experimental breeding program and discussing grazing improvements with agronomist; relaxes on his land with his horse.*

DESPITE BUSY BUSINESS SCHEDULE,
*Adams shows deepest
enthusiasm around his family:
proudly holding baby son
Stephan Stanley;
blowing out candles at
wife's birthday party;
dancing and joking with Mrs. Adams
at charity ball; and dancing
with his daughter, Stephanie,
at her birthday party.*

IN RARE MOMENTS away from
business or family,
Adams shoots low golf score
and fishes with
skill and gusto.
Adams kneels to soothe son, Gary,
over finger burned on a hot weld;
youngster grimaces and bears it.

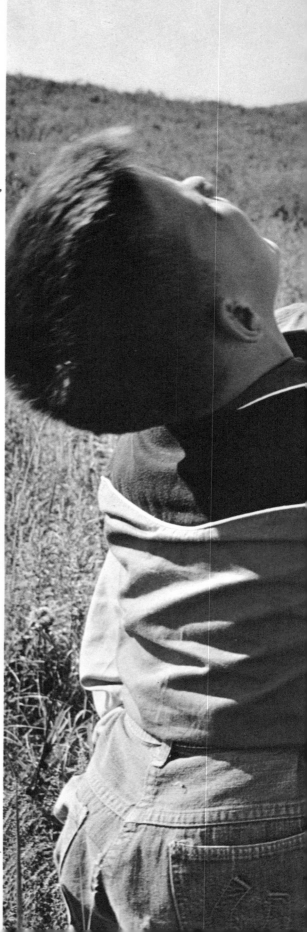

IN FAMILY PORTRAIT taken several years ago,
Boots and Dorothy Glynn beam proudly at their growing children.

was a good shot," says Hughes, "and I was angry. I threw my gun away, and it landed muzzle up in the mud. Boots started to laugh, and suddenly I knew that he'd tricked me. What he'd done was spend hours, the night before, taking all the shot out of my shells." Another time, on a deer hunt in New Mexico, Adams used a dime to twist the sight of Hughes' rifle about 75 degrees off target. "The next day we all got our bag of game," says Adams, "but Arthur shot all day and never got a thing. He even missed at 50 yards. Next morning he went out with a gun that had no telescopic sight on it, and got his deer in 30 minutes."

Another hunting experience Adams will never forget was the time he hunted geese in Mexico. "They were so thick we could lie down on our backs and shoot them. I said, 'One of these days I'm going to shoot a bird and catch it as it falls.' Then one came over and I fired and put my gun down and, sure enough, I never had to stir, it fell right in my arms, like catching a baseball."

To fulfill his wide variety of functions, Boots Adams had to draw on what was called "the main asset of Phillips Petroleum that doesn't show on the balance sheet"—his enormous energy. Despite greying hair, Adams looks much younger than his years. And except for a dangerous brush many years ago with amebic dysentery, he has always enjoyed excellent health. When in pursuit of a business deal, he can go for days with virtually no sleep; and he has the converse faculty of being able to dismiss problems from his mind and fall asleep instantly. Says Boots' physician, Dr. Frederick Campbell: "Boots has a built-in drive, along with the endocrine system to power it and sustain it. It's something like a higher-octane gasoline. And he also has the rugged physique necessary to stand up under the punishment this constant driving puts on his body."

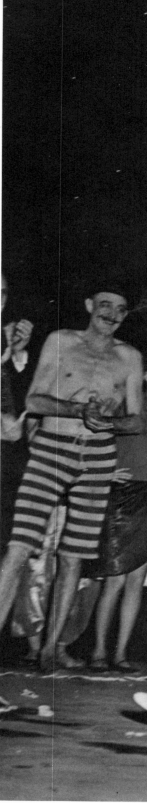

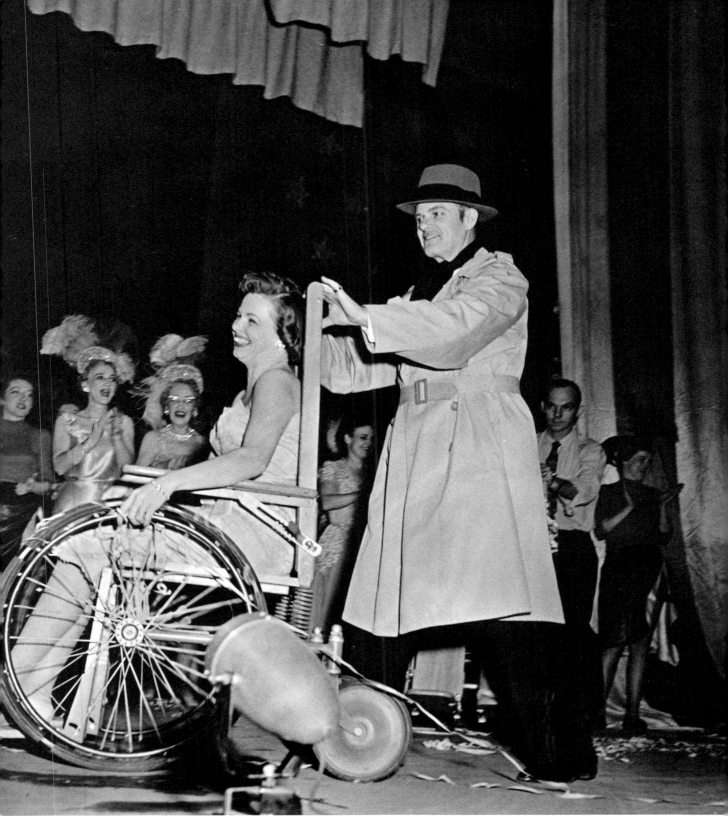

SECRET AGENT 007 *(alias Boots Adams) does some*
melodramatic acting in a skit put on to raise funds for fight on nephrosis.

110   AT THE ADAMS HOME *(shown right), most recent family portrait:*
standing, l. to r.; Mrs. Adams, Stephen Stanley (Steve),
Gary Clark, Stephanie Lyn, Kenneth Glenn (Ken);
seated, Lisa Ann and Boots.

112   THE ADAMS GRIN CAPTIVATES all in sight
as Boots cuts booted cake at 65th birthday party.
Same grin reveals lineage in the faces
of his older children by earlier marriage,
daughter Mary Louise (Mrs. John A. Hendrick),
and Kenneth (Bud) Adams, Jr.

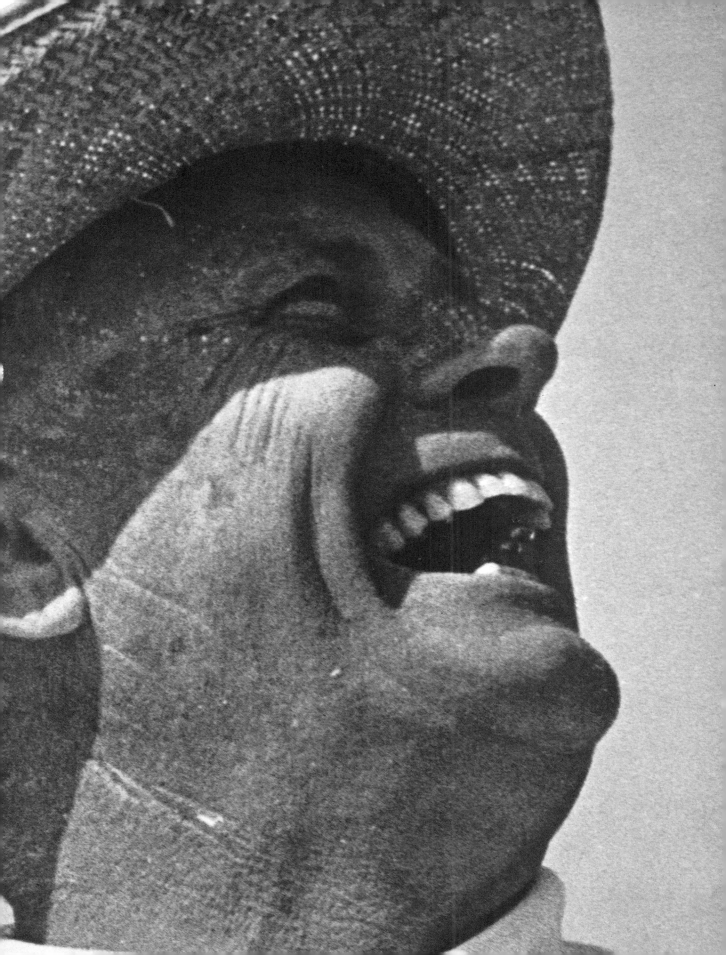

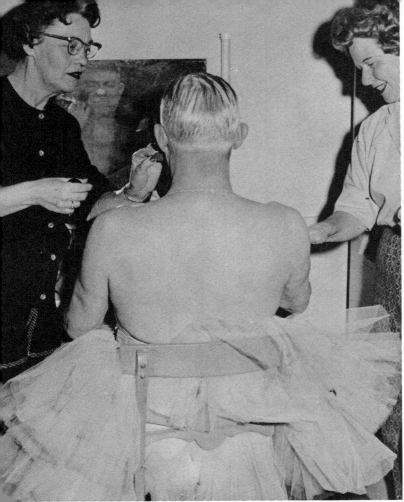

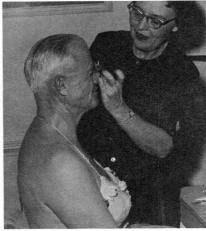

GAME FOR ANYTHING,
Boots good-naturedly gets costumed
and made up as a ballerina
for fund-raising party entertainment.
Also teams up for a comedy golf act.

Over the years, many tributes have been paid to Adams in his many roles. From these, here is a small sampling of how some of the "others" in his life have seen him:

Wyandotte, Kan., High School Yearbook: "Boots is known by his good looks and athletic prowess."

Mrs. Luella Adams: "I get to see him about once a month. He comes to Kansas City for the Federal Reserve Board meeting, but instead of having lunch at the bank he comes home to have lunch with me. He calls me once a week, even if he only has five minutes. I think that's awful nice."

L. E. Fitzjarrald, his first boss: "He would take your criticism. Once we had a pretty fair argument and he called me up and said he just wanted to thank me for setting him straight. He thought he was pretty hot stuff as a basketball player, but I never knew him to throw his weight around."

Stanley Learned, President, Phillips Petroleum Co.: "I've known Boots since 1926; I was an engineer when he was in the payroll department. We both had trouble making ends meet at that time, and because I wasn't married he used to borrow money from me, but he'd always pay it back at the end of the month . . . Three things stand out about him, then and now: his intelligence and judgment; his sense of timing in making deals; and his willingness to learn."

John J. Kettle, Dallas, Texas, banker-friend: "Boots has always been an optimist."

Harry Darby, Kansas City, Kan., industrialist and former U. S. Senator: "He set his goals early in life and worked hard to attain them. He's a gambler: he knows when to take a chance, and is always ready to do so. A great mind—a great heart—one of the best that big business offers."

C. R. Musgrave, former Phillips Petroleum vice-president: "Frank Phillips built the foundation of this company, and Ken Adams put the building on it."

Robert Anderson, former U. S. Secretary of the Treasury: "When Boots was in Europe with me he served as the personification of the American system of free enterprise. His openness and enthusiasm, and the Horatio Alger quality of his own life story, had a tremendous effect on European and Asian business and political leaders."

Dr. Frederick B. Campbell: "Adams is the only person I ever saw successfully do that trick in which you manipulate a labyrinth box to move a marble from one end to the other of an 'obstacle course.' It demonstrated

116

APPLAUSE FOR PUBLIC SERVICE *contributions is expressed in honorary Doctor of Laws degree conferred by Oklahoma Baptist University*

his high degree of patience, coordination, concentration, quick reflexes. ... He has that indefinable something that makes an individual stand out from the crowd. Wouldn't it be nice if we could isolate some of that substance and inject it into a portion of our population?"

An editorial in the Tulsa World, April 30, 1964: "If there is a single Oklahoman who does not recognize the great contributions Adams has made to his state, his nation and his firm, we do not know who it could be. It has been Adams who nurtured his company to its position as the eighth largest integrated oil, chemical and mineral complex in the nation in less than 50 years. Yet Adams has been more than an executive leader in petroleum. He has been a close and firm influence in the cultural and political life of Oklahoma—an influence even more far-reaching, perhaps, than some of our more famous figures of the past."

Osage Indian Tribal Council, upon inducting Adams as an honorary member of the tribe on Oct. 16, 1952: "We give Kenneth Adams the Indian name, *Ses-sah-moie*. This means, 'Leader of Men.'"

BOOTS' MANY ACTIVITIES
gain him frequent tributes.
He is adopted into Osage tribe
and named Seh-sah-moie,
Leader of Men;
earns scroll for work in Jesters;
and plaque for his services
to the Bartlesville
American Legion Post.

Looking Ahead at 66

MOST MEN, AT 65, AND WITH 45 YEARS OF SERVICE to one company, would be ready to call it a career, to retire and to reminisce. Not so Boots Adams. This book, perhaps, represents about as much of a concession as he is yet ready to make toward the remembrance of things past. His eye is still on the future. And the future looks as challenging and rewarding as it did when he first sat down at his warehouse desk in the fall of 1920.

One future he looks forward to is that of his own industry: "There are as many opportunities in the field today as there were 10 or 20 or 40 years ago. When I started, all our company did was produce and sell oil and gas. Then we got into refining and transporting and marketing. Now the petrochemical end of the business is booming—and it's going to end up being between twice or three times as big as the rest of everything put together."

The other future is his own. Recently Adams said: "Like any other person, my number one interest is my family. All my thinking and all my desire is to be helpful to them. But naturally the company is my second love. I can't imagine I will ever quit wanting to do whatever I can to help it continue to grow."

Upon his retirement as an employee in 1964 at the mandatory age of 65, Adams retained his titles as Chairman of the Board and Chairman of the Finance Committee. In these positions he feels his most constructive functions can be to give the benefit of his experience to top management without, as Adams puts it, "getting in the way of the people who are running the company."

Says Adams: "Retirement to me is not the conventional idea of retirement. To me, retirement opens up all sorts of opportunities to keep as busy as I have been all along. And I'm just as happy as a bird dog full of fleas." There's a story about Boots that highlights this attitude of his toward the future. A Phillips executive, out of town to negotiate a delicate and complex deal, called Adams to report. He started to tell what had happened during the day. Adams cut him short:
"I don't give a damn what happened today," he said. "What'll happen tomorrow?"
At 66, that's still Kenneth Adams' credo, still what he asks of himself and of life:

What'll happen tomorrow?

TRANSITION OF LEADERSHIP.
Smiles of confidence wreath faces of Board Chairman Adams, and Stanley Learned, President and new Chief Executive Officer.

WHILE HIS MOUNT GRAZES *by peaceful lake, Boots Adams reflects as he looks toward a personal future of ever-broadening horizons.*

Chronology

August 31, 1899	*Born in Horton, Kansas; of Scotch-Irish-Dutch-German stock*
1903	*Family moved to 75 South Valley, Kansas City, Kansas; flood refugees sheltered by Adams family gave small Kenneth Stanley his nickname because of his new black boots with red tops.*
1917	*Graduated from Wyandotte High School (Kansas City); matriculated at University of Kansas; worked in grocery, drug store, print shop, on farm, and sold aluminum ware.*
1918	*U. S. Army; Officers' Candidate School, Field Artillery, Camp Zachary Taylor, Louisville, Kentucky.*
1920	*Fresh from the University of Kansas campus to Bartlesville for a job on ice-wagon.*
November 17, 1920	*Joined Phillips Petroleum Company as a $125-per-month clerk in the warehouse-material department.*
1921	*Organized and played on the first employee basketball team, inaugurating an outstanding continuous program of AAU competition (elected in 1958 to Helms Athletic Foundation's Basketball Hall of Fame).*
1922	*Transferred to the production department where he became assistant to the operations manager.*
1926	*Transferred to accounting department where he became assistant chief clerk; pursued extension and correspondence courses in accounting, business administration and banking.*
1927	*Named Assistant Secretary of the Company.*
1928	*Became Assistant Secretary and Assistant Treasurer when he transferred to the treasury department; was a member of the company's executive staff from this time until retirement.*
1932	*Chosen at age 32, by founder and president Frank Phillips to fill the newly created position of Assistant to the President.*
1932	*Set up and headed the new Budget and Operating Committee.*
1935	*Assumed additional office of Treasurer; also became a member of the Board of Directors and Executive Committee.*
January 1, 1938	*Became Executive Vice President.*
April, 1938	*Elected President at age 38, one of the nation's youngest corporation heads.*

Early 1940's	*Directed huge expansion and diversification program and Phillips' entry into the petrochemical field during crucial years of World War II, following by fertilizers, plastics, atomic energy ventures.*
1949	*Became Chief Executive Officer upon retirement of Frank Phillips.*
November 20, 1950	*Banquet recognizing Mr. Adams' 30-year Phillips service and marking completion of the Adams Building named in his honor.*
April 24, 1951	*Elected Chairman of the Board of Directors.*
1953	*Company assets, $1 billion; Mr. Adams had led the company into industry's most exclusive "fraternity."*
April 28, 1964	*At Mr. Adams' request, Phillips President Learned was designated Chief Executive Officer; Mr. Adams continued as Chairman of the Board and was selected Chairman of the newly created Finance Committee.*
September 1, 1964	*Retired as a Phillips employee but continued as Board Chairman and Finance Committee Chairman.*

Selected Honors and Awards

1944	*Chairman, District No. 2 Production Committee, Petroleum Administration for War (followed by directorship, National Petroleum Council).*
1945	*Coroneted 33° Mason (also is a Knight Templar, Shriner and a member of the Royal Order of Jesters).*
1946	*Named a "Significant Sig" by the National Council of Sigma Chi, the fraternity's highest alumni honor.*
1949	*Director and Member of the Executive Committee, American Petroleum Institute.*
1949	*Elected to the 25-Year Club of the Petroleum Industry.*
1951	*President, Bartlesville Chamber of Commerce.*
1952	*Honorary member of the Osage Indian Nation; given the name of "Ses-sah-moie" (Leader of Men); was the second person to be so honored by the tribe, Frank Phillips being the first.*
1952	*Oklahoma Outstanding American Legionnaire Award (was Commander of the Bartlesville post in 1927).*
1953	*Elected to the Legion of Honor and Supreme Council of the Order of DeMolay.*
1954 and recurring years	*Elected Member of the Board, 10th District Federal Reserve Bank of Kansas City.*
1955	*Received the Distinguished Alumni Award, University of Kansas and its Alumni Association. Also Honorary Doctor of Laws degree, Drury College, Springfield, Missouri.*
1958	*General Grand Chapter Award of the Royal Arch Masons.*
1958	*Inducted into the Oklahoma Hall of Fame.*
1958	*Special guest at annual meeting of Board of Directors of the World Bank in New Delhi, India.*
1959	*Honorary Doctor of Laws degree, Oklahoma Baptist University, Shawnee.*
1960	*Distinguished Service Medal, Royal Arch Masons.*
1960	*Distinguished Service Citation, University of Oklahoma.*
Numerous years	*Has served on the Board of Directors, Mid-Continent Oil & Gas Association and Independent Petroleum Association of America; Member-at-Large, Cherokee Area Council of Boy Scouts of America; has also been active in Oklahoma Medical Research Foundation, Masonic Charity Foundation of America, various cattlemen's associations and sponsored work done by 4-H and FFA boys and girls.*